NATIONAL GEOGRAPHIC

Ladders

LET'S KEEP MOVING

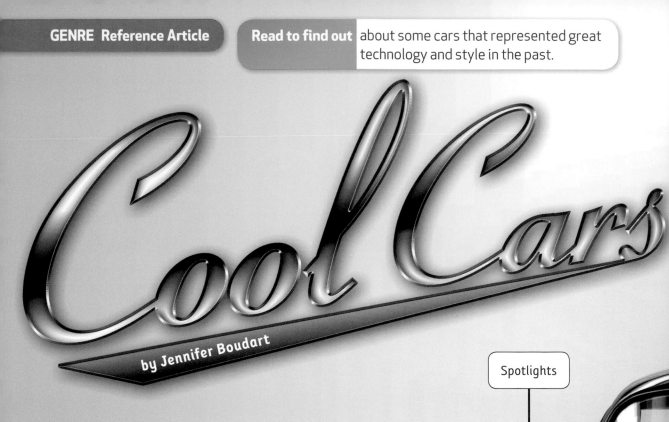

Cool Cars

by Jennifer Boudart

Spotlights

Inventors began creating automobiles, or cars, in the late 1800s. Back then, cars were basically "horseless carriages." But big changes would come in the 1940s, 50s, and 60s. Let's look at some features of cars that made them safe, affordable, and, well, cool!

The company said the car was named for the strength of the pilgrims at Plymouth Rock. The hood ornament still sported a ship, the Mayflower, like the 1942 model. But now the hood ornament lit up.

Farmers used a kind of string called Plymouth twine to bind hay. Legend says the car was given the same well-known name so farmers would buy it.

1947
PLYMOUTH DELUXE SEDAN

When World War II ended, automakers began making cars again. The public was eager to buy new models. Yet automakers could not afford to invest in new car designs. Factories had been turning out airplanes and tanks during the war. So Chrysler Corporation updated their 1942 models with a few new features. New grilles, headlights, and hood ornaments made buyers think they were getting a different car.

A gas cap covered the fuel tank, which held about 53 liters (14 gallons) of fuel.

The car's brakes responded to lighter foot pressure and slowed the car more quickly than brake systems on other cars.

Speedometer

Clock

Extra-large steering wheel

1956
Cadillac Eldorado Seville

Cadillac was the go-to luxury car company in the fifties. Cadillac specialized in flashy cars. Its cars had lots of chrome, eye-catching lines, and powerful engines. Cadillac became a leader in luxury car sales during the 1950s. In 1956, Cadillac released a model called the Eldorado Seville. The Eldorado had extensive chrome trim, stylish tail fins, and an extra-powerful engine. Its popularity helped Cadillac move up from 10th to 9th place in sales of American-made cars.

The Eldorado's tail fins were longer and taller than any other model released in 1956.

The gas cap was hidden in a taillight.

The Eldorado's tail fins looked a bit like shark fins, and they became even bigger in later models. They actually improved handling by making the car more **aerodynamic**. The aerodynamic shape allowed air to flow around the car so the car was easier to steer and used less gas. The fins also helped steady the car at higher speeds.

Speedometer

Clock

Gearshift

Treated glass gave windows a green tint that filtered sunlight. The result was a safer, cooler ride.

An automatic headlight dimmer detected light from oncoming cars. Light triggered an **electric current** that flipped a dimming switch. The Eldorado's lights dimmed until the other car passed. Then they brightened again. Dimmed headlights didn't bother oncoming drivers.

Buyers could choose a gold-plated grille. Bullet-shaped bumper guards offered protection as well as style.

The Eldorado's spoked wheels came with silver or gold plating.

In Spanish, the words "el dorado" mean "the golden one."

1966
FORD MUSTANG CONVERTIBLE

More people bought a Mustang in 1966 than in any other year it has been sold. The younger generation of that day liked the Mustang because it was so different from earlier cars. Mustangs were exotic and they had plenty of design options. Ford offered three models: a coupe, a fastback, and a convertible. Mustang owners could create a custom car by choosing the paint color, wheel style, and engine size.

The 1966 grille showed the running mustang against horizontal chrome bars for a sleek look.

The wheels' racecar-style covers pleased buyers.

The Mustang has been produced every year since it was introduced in 1964.

The Mustang's design and logo inspired a new car style called "pony cars," with long hoods and short back ends. And they could go fast. With some engines, Mustangs hit speeds up to 135 miles per hour.

The one-millionth Mustang rolled off the assembly line on March 2, 1966.

People could order one of 23 colors. They included Candy Apple Red, Raven Black, and Springtime Yellow.

Speedometer

Racecar-style steering wheel

Gearshift

Check In How were these three classic cars similar and different?

FLIGHT AROUND THE GLOBE

by Judy Elgin Jensen

On March 23, 2007, Barrington Irving entered the cockpit of an airplane named *Inspiration.* He was about to fly into history. Eight years earlier, 15-year-old Irving dreamed of playing college football. When a pilot suggested a career in **aviation,** Irving said he wasn't smart enough. But the pilot invited Irving aboard an airplane, and the young man was hooked.

Instead of taking a football scholarship, Irving worked to earn money. He spent time at the airport and played video games to practice flight skills. Then Irving earned a college scholarship to study aviation science. During his senior year, Irving's new dream took shape.

BARRINGTON IRVING is a pilot and an educator. In 2007, at age 23, Irving became the youngest person and first African American to fly solo around the globe. Irving also founded "Experience Aviation," an organization that teaches students about aviation.

Irving wanted to be the youngest person to fly solo around the world. His dream seemed impossible. Irving was only 20 years old, and no one younger than the mid-thirties had ever done it. Plus, Irving had no money and no airplane!

Irving hoped sponsors would lend him an airplane, but companies kept turning him down. They thought he would fail, given his age. Then one company agreed to build a plane for free if Irving provided the materials. After two years, he received his first donation: a free engine. Piece by piece, Irving made his plane a reality. He collected $300,000 worth of donated parts for a fast and fuel-efficient plane. He named it *Inspiration*.

While *Inspiration* was being built, Irving learned all about its operation. Most pilots attempting such a trip would have had over 10,000 flight hours. Irving had only 600. He practiced flying over mountains and oceans. He spent a year planning his stops in many countries, where he'd refuel and meet local people. Finally, 23-year-old Irving took off from Miami, Florida.

This airplane is similar to Irving's plane, *Inspiration*.

FUEL The tanks are housed in the wings. They hold about 200 liters (53 gallons) in each wing.

MATERIALS The plane is made of very light materials to reduce the **force** needed to move it through the air.

PROPELLER The motion of the blades pulls the plane through the air.

SHAPE The covers over the wheels are one of the features that make the plane more **aerodynamic.** This feature helps it fly faster on less fuel than other similar planes.

Inside the Cockpit

GAUGES Energy stored in a battery creates an **electric current** that runs lights, flight instruments, and a radio. The gauges help the pilot know if all the systems are working.

Irving hoped to return to Miami in 41 days, but he soon faced challenges. Heavy snows delayed him for two weeks in Canada. From there, Irving flew nine hours over the ocean to the Azores. He flew *Inspiration* high to avoid storms because he had no weather radar and de-icing systems. No one had donated this equipment, and Irving couldn't afford it. He hit a sandstorm while flying over Saudi Arabia. Had sand clogged the engine, he could have crashed!

Irving battled loneliness and fatigue from sitting in a cramped cockpit for hours and flying on little sleep. At each stop, Irving updated his blog, where 300,000 students tracking *Inspiration* could see pictures. He also met fans and local officials. On a 12-hour flight from Japan to Alaska, powerful storms rocked the plane and limited visibility. Still, Irving arrived safely. A few weeks later, on June 27, Irving landed back in Miami. He'd been gone 97 days.

CANADA

UNITED STATES

Azores (Portugal)

SPAIN ITALY

JAPAN

EGYPT

UNITED ARAB EMIRATES

INDIA

THAILAND

PACIFIC OCEAN

PACIFIC OCEAN

ATLANTIC OCEAN

INDIAN OCEAN

N
W   E
S

0   2,000   4,000 Miles

0   2,000 4,000 Kilometers

Irving flew about 48,000 kilometers (30,000 miles). The map names some of the countries he stopped in.

Inspiring Others

Irving was inspired by the young people he met while planning his trip. In 2005, he founded Experience Aviation to teach young people about careers in math and science. Students attend camps where they can build airplanes and meet aviation professionals. What's next? Irving is turning a jet into a flying classroom. Students will follow online as Irving flies around the world once again.

Check In   What challenges did Irving overcome to make his dream come true?

The Space Shuttle

1981–2011

by Jennifer Boudart

It's a rocket! It's a plane! It's a giant space taxi! Actually, it's all three. The space shuttle is a reusable **spacecraft** built by the National Aeronautics and Space Administration (NASA). It launched like a rocket, landed like an airplane, and moved people and materials high above Earth.

Columbia sits on Launch Pad 39A in March 1981. Everything is being readied for its first flight.

NASA sent five shuttles on 134 missions from 1981 to 2011. Hundreds of people orbited Earth this way. They ran investigations, studied Earth, and even helped build a space station. Let's meet the shuttles!

ENTERPRISE (1976–1979)
Full-sized test vehicle used for flight tests in the atmosphere and on the ground.

COLUMBIA (1979–2003)
Missions: 28
Distance Flown: 195,852,325 km (121,696,993 mi.)
Total Passengers: 159

CHALLENGER (1982–1986)
Missions: 10
Distance Flown: 38,079,155 km (23,661,290 mi.)
Total Passengers: 60

DISCOVERY (1983–2011)
Missions: 39
Distance Flown: 238,539,663 km (148,221,675 mi.)
Total Passengers: 222

ATLANTIS (1985–2011)
Missions: 32
Distance Flown: 194,168,813 km (120,650,907 mi.)
Total Passengers: 191

ENDEAVOUR (1991–2011)
Missions: 25
Distance Flown: 197,761,262 km (122,883,151 mi.)
Total Passengers: 145

Mission Milestones

September 17
1976

Enterprise rolls off the assembly line. It never flew in space, but it supplied parts for shuttles that did.

February 7
1984

Two astronauts aboard *Challenger* took the first untethered spacewalk. Bruce McCandless II and Robert L. Stewart floated freely for six hours! They used jet packs on their spacesuits to steer themselves.

January 28
1986

Challenger exploded after launching. The shuttle and its seven-person crew were lost.

October 18
1989

From space, *Atlantis* launched the first spacecraft to Jupiter. The unmanned spacecraft, named *Galileo*, entered Jupiter's orbit six years later.

April 12
1981

Columbia launched NASA's first space shuttle mission. The two astronauts aboard flew just over 1.6 million kilometers (1 million miles) and orbited Earth 37 times.

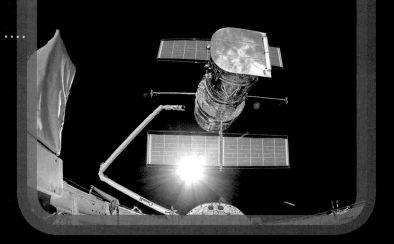

April 25
1990

Discovery launched the Hubble Space Telescope. Since then, the telescope has viewed black holes and far-off galaxies. Space shuttles have visited the telescope a number of times to make repairs.

February 1
2003

Columbia broke apart while returning to Earth. The shuttle and its seven-person crew were lost.

October 29
1998

Aboard *Discovery*, John Glenn became the oldest person in space at age 77. In 1962, he was the first U.S. astronaut to orbit Earth.

February 11
2000

An international crew blasted off aboard *Endeavour*. They used radar antennas to make a three-dimensional map of Earth's surface. The radar mapped about 80 percent of Earth's surface, such as this mountain range in Russia. It took four years to analyze the pictures!

July 21
2011

Atlantis launched a satellite that would test new solar technology. When the shuttle glided back to Earth, the shuttle era ended.

Building a New Place in Space

The International Space Station (ISS) is the largest spacecraft ever built. It's the size of a football field and weighs almost 450,000 kilograms (1,000,000 pounds). It's made up of linking pieces called modules. Agencies from 15 countries spent 12 years building it.

Russia sent the first ISS module into space in 1998. A few weeks later, *Endeavour* brought a second module to connect to the first one. Then rockets and other shuttles traveled to the ISS. From 1998 to 2011, *Discovery, Endeavour,* and *Atlantis* made 37 trips. They moved supplies, parts, and crew members.

∧ Astronauts make repairs to the ISS in February 2011.

Solar panels convert sunlight into electricity. Together, all of the solar panels make up about three-fourths of the total size of the ISS. The array supplies the **electric current** needed to run the ISS's systems.

The ISS's shape does not have to be **aerodynamic** because at high Earth orbit, there's not enough air to affect its flight.

This May 2011 photo of *Endeavour* was taken by a Russian cosmonaut aboard another spacecraft that had just left the ISS.

ISS

- Up to six people live on board the ISS at all times. They zoom around the planet once every 90 minutes, studying space and Earth.

- The ISS modules include places to sleep, eat, and even exercise. They also have laboratories for experiments and areas for computer controls and docking.

- The shuttles carried robotic arms that were mounted onto the ISS. The robotic arms helped build the ISS. Now, the robotic arms move astronauts around while they operate science experiments.

Mission Accomplished

On July 8, 2011, *Atlantis* left NASA's Kennedy Space Center. Four crew members along with supplies headed for the ISS. The work was routine, but the mission was not. In fact, it was NASA's last space shuttle flight. After 30 years of working in Earth's orbit, NASA wanted to send astronauts further into space, where the space shuttles could not go. The ISS was fully operational. Spacecraft from around the world would supply it now.

Atlantis safely docked at the ISS two days later. For eight days, crews from both spacecrafts transferred the supplies from *Atlantis* to the ISS. President Barack Obama phoned to congratulate everyone. *Atlantis* separated from the ISS a final time, and after launching one last satellite, touched down on July 21, 2011. *Atlantis*, and the other space shuttles, were home to stay.

The pilot moves flaps on the wings down to land *Atlantis*. The flaps squeeze the water vapor in the air, and this causes the water vapor to turn into liquid water. So the curly trails from the wings are like clouds.

∧ *Atlantis'* home is at the Kennedy Space Center. You can tour *Atlantis* at the Visitor Complex.

A New Mission

The shuttles no longer fly, but they're still working at their final homes as tools for learning about space. Visit!

• **ATLANTIS** Kennedy Space Center Visitor's Complex (Kennedy Space Center, Florida)

• **DISCOVERY** National Air and Space Museum, Steven F. Udvar-Hazy Center (Chantilly, Virginia)

• **ENDEAVOUR** California Science Center (Los Angeles, California)

• **ENTERPRISE** Intrepid Sea, Air & Space Museum Complex (New York City, New York)

Check In   How did space shuttles help space exploration?

NEXT STOP MA

Martian soil has red iron oxide. This is why Mars is nicknamed the red planet. Winds whip up giant clouds of red dust that surround the planet.

by Judy Elgin Jensen

MARS

Is life possible on Mars?

Maybe. Scientists are trying to find
out. Mars is our closest planetary
neighbor. In some ways it's like Earth.
Mars and Earth have about the same
amount of dry land. Their atmospheres
are made up of similar gases, though
Martian air contains deadly amounts
of carbon dioxide. Both planets have
seasons and a similar day length. Mars
has volcanoes, canyons, and ice caps just
like those on Earth. Earth's environment
supports life, so what about Mars?
Scientists think Mars may once have
had liquid water. Water may still remain
deep underground. If so, microscopic life
may have existed on Mars in the past,
or may even exist today. The National
Aeronautic and Space Administration
(NASA) is exploring Mars for evidence of
life. NASA's *Curiosity Rover*, a mobile science
lab, has been trekking across Mars since
August 5, 2012.

THE LONG ROAD TO LIFTOFF

Curiosity is not the first NASA rover to land on Mars, but it's the most high-tech. It's bigger and more mobile than the others, and it carries many scientific instruments. NASA spent 10 years preparing for *Curiosity*'s mission.

Engineers had to build *Curiosity* and a **spacecraft** to carry it. Scientists had to calculate a landing date when Earth and Mars would align. This happens only every 26 months! Scientists also had to chart a course through space. The trip would take 254 days and cover 566,500,000 kilometers (352,000,000 miles). And where and how would *Curiosity* set down? NASA had never landed a car-sized rover before. Launch day came on November 26, 2011, and emotions were running high.

READY...

Technicians work on Curiosity at a laboratory in California. They must not contaminate the rover with germs. They don't want Earth germs carried to Mars.

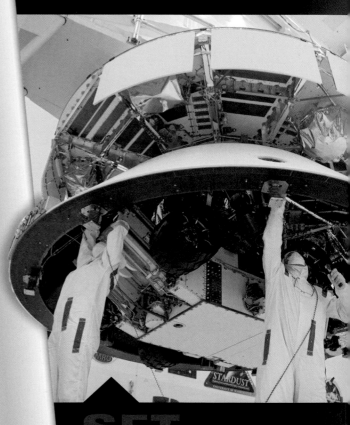

SET...

Workers pack Curiosity and its spacecraft inside a protective cone before placing it atop a rocket.

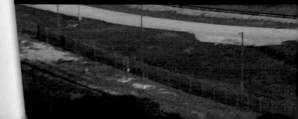

A Kansas 6th-grader won an essay contest. She named *Curiosity* and signed the rover!

GO!

A rocket carrying *Curiosity* lifts off from Florida's Cape Canaveral Air Force Station on November 26, 2011. The spacecraft carrying *Curiosity* breaks away about 45 minutes later.

THE JOURNEY

Curiosity was on its way! For nine months, scientists monitored the spacecraft and kept it on track. Finally, the spacecraft reached Mars' outer atmosphere. It was time for the entry, descent and landing (EDL) phase. Previous rovers had been dropped to Mars, but *Curiosity* was too big to drop. NASA was trying a new method, but they were scared it wouldn't work and the huge amount of money that had been spent on the mission would be wasted!

Friction slowed *Curiosity* as it entered Mars' atmosphere. Then, a giant parachute opened at the back of the spacecraft, slowing it more. Next, the protective heat shield popped off. *Curiosity* was still tucked inside the back half of the spacecraft. It was connected to a sky crane with rockets to control its own speed and direction. The sky crane ejected next and fired up its rockets. About six stories above the surface, the crane lowered *Curiosity*. The rover's wheels touched down, and the sky crane flew off. *Curiosity* landed right on target, in an area called Gale Crater.

NASA could only wait to see if their landing method worked. They called this time the "7 Minutes of Terror."

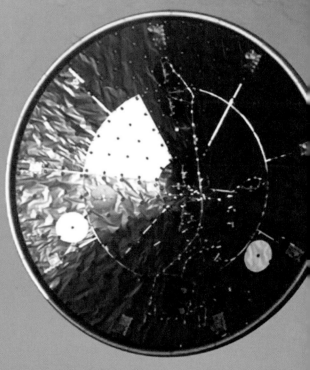

A camera on *Curiosity* took this photo of the heat shield dropping away. The 7 Minutes of Terror was about over!

A satellite orbiting Mars took this photo of the parachute slowing down *Curiosity*.

The spacecraft entered Mars' atmosphere traveling 21,000 kilometers per hour (13,000 miles per hour). It slowed down as it met friction from the atmosphere. But friction also caused intense heating. Would *Curiosity* land safely?

Spacecraft enters atmosphere
21,000 kph (13,000 mph)
125 km (78 mi.) above surface

Sky crane and
Curiosity drop away
290 kph (180 mph)
1.5 km (1 mi.)
above surface

Parachute opens
1,700 kph (1050 mph)
10 km (6 mi.) above surface

Heat shield thrown off
576 kph (358 mph)
7 km (4 mi.) above surface

Sky crane lowers *Curiosity*
1.7 kph (1 mph)
20 m (65 ft.) above surface

Curiosity released on touchdown
Sky crane flies off and crashes

NASA scientists believe Gale Crater may have once contained water. It might still have traces of water and carbon, a mineral needed for life. After a few weeks of testing, scientists took *Curiosity* on its first drive. Scientists are now directing *Curiosity* to collect and test samples from the soil and atmosphere.

Curiosity is the first rover able to test samples on site. Ten scientific instruments and 17 cameras help the rover do its work. Take a look at this drawing of how *Curiosity* would look on Mars' surface. Then read on to compare this drawing with *Curiosity's* self-portrait.

CURIOSITY: A CLOSER LOOK

LENGTH: 3 M (10 FT.)

ARM REACH: 2.2 M (7 FT.)

WEIGHT: 910 KG (2,000 LBS.)

WIDTH: 2.7 M (9 FT.)

HEIGHT: 2.2 M (7 FT.)

**TOP SPEED: 4 CM (1.5 IN.)
PER SECOND**

ANTENNA

BODY

POWER SOURCE

NEUTRON DETECTOR

Curiosity will explore Mars for about two years.

WHEELS

SIX WHEELS on jointed "legs" allow *Curiosity* to climb slopes and roll over big rocks. By locking five of the wheels, *Curiosity* can use the sixth to dig below the surface.

A **ROBOTIC ARM** scoops up rocks and soil and delivers it for testing. It also has magnifying and X-ray equipment to study minerals in each sample.

The **MAST** uses six cameras to "see" its path.

Four pairs of **HAZCAMS** watch out for hazards.

The **CHEMCAM** uses a laser to burn tiny holes in rocks and soil. The way a sample burns shows the chemicals it contains.

A **POWER SOURCE** changes heat into energy that is stored in batteries. The batteries then create **electric current** for the rover's systems.

A **WEATHER STATION** records weather conditions and the amount of ultraviolet radiation from the sun.

An **OBSERVATION TRAY** gives tools on the robotic arm a place to examine samples.

A **NEUTRON DETECTOR** checks for water in rocks and soil.

An **ANTENNA** allows for communication with scientists on Earth.

Inside the **BODY,** computers monitor all of the systems in the rover.

MAST

CHEMCAM

WEATHER STATION

ROBOTIC ARM

HAZCAMS

OBSERVATION TRAY

Curiosity sent more than 23,000 images back to Earth in its first 16 weeks.

Here is *Curiosity's* self-portrait. The camera on the rover's robotic arm took more than 50 pictures from different positions. The pictures were then combined to create a single image.

EARLY DISCOVERIES

Curiosity's early tests ran smoothly. First, the rover collected sand samples from an area called Rocknest. Its robotic arm also blasted a rock with its laser beam and analyzed the dust. *Curiosity* then started moving. It discovered an ancient streambed and a huge, distant dust storm. Instruments inside the rover further analyzed samples.

Curiosity identified traces of water in the sand. When heated, the sand also formed a chemical containing a tiny amount of carbon. Carbon is a building block for life. However, scientists don't know how this carbon got into the soil. The rover continues to inch toward its main target, a mountain named Mount Sharp. Scientists can hardly wait to see what awaits *Curiosity* there!

SLOW BUT SURE—123 DAYS, 598 M (1,961 FT.)

BRADBURY LANDING

YELLOW-KNIFE BAY

ROCKNEST

POINT LAKE

YELLOWKNIFE BAY

SOL 123

SHALER

METERS
0 5 10   20

Scientists track *Curiosity's* path on photographic maps like this. You can, too! They're on the NASA website.

Check In How was *Curiosity* engineered to travel across Mars' surface?

Discuss

1. What connections can you make among the four pieces in *Let's Keep Moving*?

2. What surprised you about the design and technology of the early cars?

3. Which piece contained the most complex problem? How did the scientists attempt to solve it? Why was it so difficult?

4. What have we learned from *Curiosity* so far? What more do scientists hope to learn?

5. What do you still wonder about ways people get from one place to another? What would be some good ways to find more information?